ISBN 978-0-260-51532-2
PIBN 11122550

English
Français
Deutsche
Italiano
Español
Português

www.forgottenbooks.com

Mythology Photography **Fiction**
Fishing Christianity **Art** Cooking
Essays Buddhism Freemasonry
Medicine **Biology** Music **Ancient
Egypt** Evolution Carpentry Physics
Dance Geology **Mathematics** Fitness
Shakespeare **Folklore** Yoga Marketing
Confidence Immortality Biographies
Poetry **Psychology** Witchcraft
Electronics Chemistry History **Law**
Accounting **Philosophy** Anthropology
Alchemy Drama Quantum Mechanics
Atheism Sexual Health **Ancient History**
Entrepreneurship Languages Sport
Paleontology Needlework Islam
Metaphysics Investment Archaeology
Parenting Statistics Criminology
Motivational

Historic, archived document

Do not assume content reflects current
scientific knowledge, policies, or practices.

FOR RELEASE
AUG. 20, P. M.

THE Wool SITUATION

BUREAU OF AGRICULTURAL ECONOMICS
UNITED STATES DEPARTMENT OF AGRICULTURE

TWS-16   BAE   JULY 1951

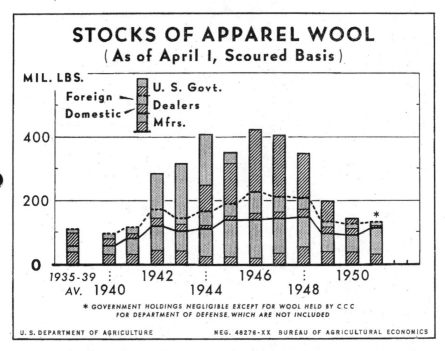

STOCKS OF APPAREL WOOL
(As of April I, Scoured Basis)

MIL. LBS.

Foreign — U. S. Govt.
Domestic — Dealers
Mfrs.

400

200

0

1935-39 : 1942 : 1946 : 1950
AV. 1940   1944   1948

* GOVERNMENT HOLDINGS NEGLIGIBLE EXCEPT FOR WOOL HELD BY C.C.C
FOR DEPARTMENT OF DEFENSE. WHICH ARE NOT INCLUDED

U. S. DEPARTMENT OF AGRICULTURE   NEG. 48276-XX   BUREAU OF AGRICULTURAL ECONOMICS

Stocks of apparel wool held by the United States Government, dealers, and mills at the end of the first quarter of this year were the lowest for that time of year since 1941. Although holdings were almost one-third larger than the 1935-39 average, they were lower relative to the rate of consumption. Stocks on April 1 represented about 17 weeks of consumption at the then current rate compared with an average of 21 weeks for 1935-39 and the peak of 37 weeks in 1946.

Commodity Credit Corporation holdings reached a peak of 230 million pounds as of the third quarter of 1946. CCC holdings had been liquidated by the end of the first quarter of this year. No wool has been or is likely to be purchased by the CCC under the 1951 support program, since market prices have been and are expected to continue above support levels.

The Defense Supplies Corporation stockpile, which was built up during the early war years, reached a peak of 183 million pounds at the beginning of 1944. The last of these wools were disposed of during 1945.

STATISTICAL SUMMARY

Item	Unit	PRICES								Last date available as percent of a year earlier
		1950				1951				
		Mar.	Apr.	May	June	Mar.	Apr.	May	June	
Price received by farmers	Cents	49.6	53.2	55.4	57.6	+ 119.0	113.0	106.0	101.0	175
Parity price	Cents	50.2	50.2	50.9	51.3	56.3	56.9	56.7	56.9	111
Farm as percent of parity	Percent	99	106	109	112	211	199	187	178	
Boston market price: 1/										
Domestic wool										
Territory, scoured basis	Cents									
64s, 70s, 80s, staple	per	162.5	162.9	169.8	176.0	375.0	333.8	313.0	285.0	162
56s, combing	pound	118.4	120.2	128.5	139.5	310.0	266.2	242.0	220.0	158
Bright fleece, grease basis										
64s, 70s, 80s, delaine	do.	64.0	64.2	67.4	71.0	146.1	130.2	120.6	110.0	155
56s, combing	do.	57.0	56.4	62.0	67.8	156.4	132.5	123.6	112.5	166
Foreign wool, excl. duty										
Australian, clean basis										
64s, 70s, topmaking	do.	157.5	160.0	171.5	177.5	360.0	327.5	301.0	282.5	
Montevideo, grease basis										
56s, (Is)	do.	68.4	70.0	77.0	79.0	217.5	191.2	163.0	150.0	159
50s, (IIs)	do.	61.0	61.0	66.2	71.0	202.5	180.0	154.8	144.6	190
Other textile fibers										
Cotton, middling 15/16 2/	do.	31.9	32.5	32.9	33.8	45.1	45.2	45.2	45.2	134
Rayon, staple fiber										
Viscose 1½ denier	do.	35.0	35.0	35.0	35.0	40.0	40.0	40.0	40.0	114
Acetate 5 denier	do.	42.0	42.0	42.0	42.0	48.0	48.0	48.0	48.0	114

	Unit	CONSUMPTION AND SUPPLIES								
		1950				1951				
		Jan.	Feb.	Mar.	Apr.	Jan.	Feb.	Mar.	Apr. 3/	
Mill consumption 4/										
Per week during month 5/										
Scoured basis										
Apparel (domestic and duty-paid foreign)	1,000	7,838	8,671	8,346	7,777	8,051	7,414	6,986	8,557	110
Carpet (duty-free foreign)	pounds	3,929	3,931	3,953	4,163	3,318	3,312	3,179	2,583	62
Grease basis										
Carpet(duty-free foreign)	do.	5,337	5,516	5,534	5,829	4,712	4,724	4,478	3,359	58
Accumulated since January 1										
Scoured basis										
Apparel(domestic & duty-paid foreign)	Million	31.4	66.0	107.8	138.9	40.3	69.9	97.9	140.6	101
Carpet (duty-free foreign)	pounds	15.7	31.4	51.2	67.9	16.6	29.8	42.6	55.5	82
Grease basis										
Carpet (duty-free foreign)	do.	21.3	43.4	71.1	94.4	23.6	42.5	60.4	77.2	82
Imports - actual weight 6/										
Apparel wool (dutiable)	do.	45.0	37.3	32.9	22.4	49.3	35.0	51.1	52.2	233
Carpet wool (duty-free)	do.	31.9	36.6	32.7	33.5	22.5	14.5	14.8	21.5	64
Accumulated since January 1										
Apparel wool (dutiable)	do.	45.0	82.3	115.2	137.6	49.3	84.4	135.5	187.7	136
Carpet wool (duty-free)	do.	31.9	68.5	101.1	134.6	22.5	37.0	51.8	73.2	54
Imports - clean content 6/										
Apparel wool (dutiable)	do.	27.0	22.3	19.3	16.5	30.4	22.2	32.2	32.5	197
Carpet wool (duty-free)	do.	22.8	25.1	22.0	23.0	15.5	9.9	10.7	15.4	67
Accumulated since January 1										
Apparel wool (dutiable)	do.	27.0	49.3	68.5	85.0	30.4	52.6	84.7	117.3	138
Carpet wool (duty-free)	do.	22.8	47.8	69.9	92.9	14.5	25.3	36.0	51.4	55
Wool fabric production										
Accumulated since January 1										
Apparel fabrics	Million			85.3				81.8		96
Government orders	Linear			2.5				9.5		380
Men's and boy's wear	Yards			42.1				38.1		90
Women's and children's wear	do.			40.7				34.2		84
Non-apparel fabrics	do.			16.4				13.9		85
Blanketing	do.			4.3				5.0		116
Other non-apparel fabrics	do.			12.1				8.9		74
Total woven fabrics	do.			101.7				95.7		94

Compiled from official sources.
1/ P.M.A. Boston Market Reports.
2/ Average of 10 markets.
3/ Preliminary.
4/ Excludes wool consumed on the cotton and other spinning systems and in the manufacturing of felts, hat bodies, and other miscellaneous products.
5/ Monthly periods are 4 or 5 calendar weeks generally totaling 13 weeks each quarter.
6/ Imports for consumption.

T H E   W O O L   S I T U A T I O N

Approved by the Outlook and Situation Board, August 14, 1951

SUMMARY

The sharp decline in wool prices in the British Dominions which began late in March continued through the end of the season. Prices as
auctions closed late in June were 15 to 25 percent lower than when they
opened in September 1950 and 45 to 55 percent lower than the peak levels
reached in March of this year, but were still 20 to 30 percent higher
than at the end of the 1949-50 season.

Major factors in the sharp decline since March were (1) virtual
completion by late March of United States military ordering for the fiscal year; (2) a sharp reduction in demand at retail, wholesale, and manufacturing levels for civilian wool goods due to a decline in retail
sales following the heavy war-scare buying and to apparent large inventories in manufacturing and distribution channels; and (3) the greater
use of synthetic and other fibers in place of wool due to the greater increase in wool prices than in prices of these other materials.

Prices received by United States growers for shorn wool continued to
decline from the peak levels of March. The average of 86.5 cents per pound,
grease, basis, in mid-July was 14.5 cents below mid-June and 32.5 cents below the March record.

Wool prices are now somewhat below the ceilings established by OPS
Ceiling Price Regulation 35.

Since consumer incomes are expected to continue to increase, demand
for raw wool for civilian goods is likely to strengthen as inventories
are reduced to levels in line with retail sales. Military requirements
during the present fiscal year again will be substantial. At the same
time, world supply of wool probably will not be greatly different from
last season. World production is expected to be slightly above last year
and the carry-over in the major exporting countries, particularly in New
Zealand and Argentina, is larger. These increases probably will just
about offset the reduction in Joint Organization holdings and in stocks
in consuming countries. World prices next season probably will average
somewhat higher than present levels. However, government programs and
policies including the volume and scheduling of military orders, price
ceilings, etc., could be important factors.

Wool production in the United States for the current season is expected to be about 260 million pounds, grease basis, about 3 percent more than in 1950. Shorn wool production is now estimated at 229 million pounds, grease basis, about 4 percent more than last year. The lower rate of slaughter this year relative to inventories indicates that growers are continuing to build up breeding herds and that a further increase in shorn wool production is likely next year. Pulled wool production this year is likely to be slightly lower than last year.

The decline in demand for wool for civilian goods is reflected in mill consumption in the United States. In spite of the large military orders, the weekly rate of mill consumption of apparel wool on the woolen and worsted systems during the first 5 months of this year was 3 percent less than for the same months of last year. Carpet wool consumption was down 30 percent.

Imports of apparel wool during the early part of this year were substantially higher than last year. Imports for consumption during January-May exceeded those of the same months of last year by 36 percent. However, imports probably declined somewhat after May due to the sharply reduced United States buying in foreign markets.

REVIEW AND OUTLOOK

Prices Decline
in Foreign Markets

Wool auctions in the British Dominions closed for the season late in June. The opening auctions of the 1951-52 season are tentatively scheduled for early September in Australia and the Union of South Africa. Auctions have been scheduled for mid-August in New Zealand to sell the stocks of wool which accumulated in that country as a result of the suspension of auctions due to the dockworkers' strike.

Prices of wool at the closing auctions were 20 to 30 percent higher than a year earlier but 15 to 25 percent lower than the opening prices of last September and 45 to 55 percent lower than the peak prices of March of this year. In general, the decline in prices of crossbred wool was somewhat greater than for prices of merino wools. However, the net increase in prices of crossbred wools since last June is still somewhat greater than that for merino wools.

At the opening of the July series of London auctions on July 13, prices were 20 to 30 percent lower than at the close of the May series (table 1). At the close of the series on July 23 prices in general were about the same as those of the opening.

Table 1. - Prices of good fleece wools at the London auctions, in cents and pence per pound, clean basis, by months, 1948-51

Week ended 1/	Good medium fleeces		Fine Crossbred fleeces		Crossbred fleeces	
	64s-70s	64s-70s	56s	56s	46s	46s
	Cents	Pence	Cents	Pence	Cents	Pence
1948						
January 15	147.8	88.0	94.0	56.0	55.4	33.0
January 30	161.3	96.0	100.8	60.0	59.6	35.5
March 5	144.5	86.0	90.7	54.0	45.4	27.0
March 19	152.8	91.0	90.7	54.0	45.3	27.0
April 30	161.3	96.0	94.1	56.0	52.1	31.0
June 4	196.5	117.0	97.4	58.0	52.1	31.0
June 16	196.5	117.0	97.4	58.0	48.7	29.0
July 23	196.5	117.0	100.8	60.0	52.1	31.0
September 16	189.8	113.0	100.8	60.0	52.1	31.0
October 1	184.8	110.0	97.4	58.0	52.1	31.0
November 17	199.9	119.0	107.5	64.0	58.8	35.0
December 3	199.9	119.0	117.6	70.0	65.5	39.0
1949						
January 27	201.6	120.0	109.2	65.0	67.2	40.0
February 18	201.6	120.0	109.2	65.0	65.5	39.0
March 25	201.6	120.0	109.2	65.0	60.5	36.0
April 8	206.5	123.0	109.1	65.0	57.1	34.0
May 13	194.9	116.0	99.1	59.0	55.4	33.0
May 27	201.4	120.0	99.0	59.0	55.4	33.0
July 7	201.5	120.0	104.1	62.0	55.4	33.0
July 22	193.2	115.0	104.1	62.0	55.4	33.0
September 23	122.6	105.0	77.0	66.0	42.0	36.0
October 7	134.2	115.0	81.7	70.0	47.8	41.0
November 25	150.5	129.0	95.7	82.0	61.9	53.0
December 9	150.5	129.0	93.4	80.0	56.0	48.0
1950						
January 27	173.9	149.0	114.4	98.0	70.0	60.0
February 10	158.7	136.0	95.7	82.0	60.7	52.0
March 16	158.7	136.0	93.4	80.0	63.0	54.0
March 31	170.4	146.0	102.7	88.0	70.0	60.0
May 5	177.4	152.0	110.9	95.0	75.9	65.0
May 19	184.4	158.0	114.4	98.0	79.4	68.0
July 6	184.4	158.0	114.4	98.0	80.5	69.0
July 21	198.4	170.0	123.7	106.0	89.9	77.0
September 22	285.9	245.0	198.4	170.0	166.9	143.0
October 6	262.6	225.0	186.7	160.0	152.9	131.0
November 24	282.4	242.0	200.7	172.0	179.7	154.0
December 8	293.9	252.0	227.4	195.0	191.3	164.0
1951						
February 2	355.9	305.0	256.7	220.0	221.7	190.0
February 16	364.1	312.0	280.1	240.0	228.7	196.0
April 6	350.1	300.0	256.7	220.0	210.1	180.0
April 20	2/	2/	245.1	210.0	210.1	180.0
June 5	309.3	265.0	198.4	170.0	145.9	125.0
July 13	221.7	190.0	2/	2/	116.7	100.0
July 20	221.7	190.0	147.0	126.0	119.0	102.0

Compiled from Kreglinger and Fernau Market reports. Prices converted from pence to cents at current rates of exchange. 1/ Quotations are for weeks ending on dates shown, which are opening and closing weeks for each series. 2/ No quotation.

Prior to the decline, which began late in March, world wool prices had advanced continuously, except for minor interruptions, from late 1949. Major factors in the sharp rise from September 1950 to March of this year were the reduced supply, strong civilian demand, and large military takings. British mills in particular were heavy buyers late in 1950. The record prices of merino wools in March ranged from 2-1/4 to 2-1/2 times higher than last June with prices of crossbred wools up even more.

Prices Decline
in Domestic Markets

Prices of both imported and domestic wools at Boston reflect recent trends of wool prices abroad. Prices for most wools at Boston are now 35 to 50 percent below the record levels of March.

For the week ending August 3, prices of Australian fine wools at Boston were about 40 percent below the March peaks, while prices of 58s, 60s wools were down about 42 percent. During that week, Australian 64s, 70s good topmaking wool was quoted at $2.20 per pound, clean basis (American yield), in bond at Boston, compared with the peak of $3.65 prior to the decline. The price of Australian 58s, 60s combing wool declined from $3.35 to $1.95. In June 1950 these wools were quoted at $1.78 and $1.52, respectively.

Prices of domestic wools at Boston have shown a similar decline (table 2). Early in August prices were about 35 to 50 percent lower than the peak levels of March. For the week ending August 3 territory fine staple was quoted at $2.35, compared with $3.80 prior to the decline. For the same week, territory three-eighths blood combing (56s, 58s) was quoted at $1.75. This wool was quoted at $3.15 prior to the decline. In June 1950 these wools were quoted at $1.76 and $1.40, respectively.

Prices Received
by Growers

Prices received by domestic growers for shorn wool at mid-July averaged 86.5 cents per pound, grease basis. This was equivalent to 153 percent of parity. Prices received by growers averaged 119.0 cents at mid-March, a record high, and 58.6 cents in July 1950. The drop from March to July of this year reflects the sharp decline in wool prices in world markets during recent months.

Office of Price Stabilization
Regulations Relating to Wool
and Wool Products

From time to time since the General Ceiling Price Regulation was announced on January 26, 1951, the Office of Price Stabilization has issued specific regulations establishing ceiling prices for wool and wool top, wool and wool top futures, manufacturers of wool yarns and fabrics, and manufacturers and retailers of wool products. Among the regulations issued since the April Wool Situation was released are the following:

Prices of domestic shorn wools at Boston, clean basis, for week ended August 3, 1951, with comparisons

Classification	1950 June Cents	1951 Week ended Mar. 16 Cents	1951 Week ended May 18 Cents	Week ended Aug. 3 Cents	Percent change week ended August 3, 1951 from June 1950 Percent	Mar. 16 1951 Percent	May 18 1951 Percent
Graded shorn							
Territory							
Fine combing (Staple) (64s and finer)	176.0	380.0	310.0	235.0	33.5	-38.2	-24.2
Fine French combing (64s and finer)	164.4	365.0	295.0	225.0	36.9	-38.4	-23.7
Fine clothing (64s and finer)	152.2	315.0	250.0	205.0	34.4	-34.9	-18.0
1/2 Blood combing (Staple) (60s, 62s)	158.5	345.0	275.0	195.0	23.0	-43.5	-29.1
1/2 Blood French combing (60s, 62s)	144.4	325.0	265.0	185.0	28.1	-43.1	-30.2
1/2 Blood clothing (60s, 62s)	132.5	275.0	215.0	160.0	20.8	-41.8	-25.6
3/8 Blood combing (56s, 58s)	139.5	315.0	235.0	175.0	25.4	-44.4	-25.5
3/8 Blood clothing (56s, 58s)	102.5	255.0	195.0	135.0	31.7	-47.1	-30.8
1/4 Blood combing (48s, 50s)	122.5	300.0	225.0	165.0	34.7	-45.0	-26.7
Low 1/4 Blood	97.5	260.0	205.0	155.0	59.0	-40.4	-24.4
Common and Braid (44s and coarser)	92.5	255.0	195.0	155.0	67.6	-39.2	-20.5
Bright fleece							
Fine combing (Delaine) (64s and finer)	183.2	380.0	309.0	235.0	28.3	-38.2	-24.0
Fine clothing (64s and finer)	152.5	310.0	240.0	175.0	14.8	-43.6	-27.1
1/2 Blood combing (60s, 62s)	158.2	330.0	270.0	185.0	16.9	-43.9	-31.5
3/8 Blood combing (56s, 58s)	127.5	290.0	225.0	165.0	29.4	-43.1	-26.7
1/4 Blood combing (48s, 50s)	122.5	275.0	215.0	155.0	26.5	-43.6	-27.9
Low 1/4 Blood	99.4	245.0	195.0	145.0	45.9	-40.8	-25.6
Common and Braid (44s and coarser)	94.4	240.0	185.0	145.0	53.6	-39.6	-21.6
Semi-Bright fleece							
Fine combing (Staple) (64s and finer)	172.5	355.0	295.0	225.0	30.4	-36.6	-23.7
Fine clothing (64s and finer)	147.5	295.0	235.0	170.0	15.3	-42.4	-27.7
1/2 Blood combing (60s, 62s)	157.5	320.0	260.0	175.0	11.1	-45.3	-32.7
3/8 Blood combing (56s, 58s)	127.4	285.0	210.0	160.0	25.6	-43.9	-23.8
1/4 Blood combing (48s, 50s)	122.4	270.0	205.0	140.0	14.4	-48.2	-31.7
Low 1/4 Blood (46s)	99.4	235.0	185.0	140.0	40.8	-40.4	-24.3

CPR-35, issued by the Office of Price Stabilization on May 9, established dollars and cents ceilings on wool, mohair, and alpaca, and tops and noils of these fibers. It did not fix ceilings on cashmere, vicuna, camel hair, carpet wool, wool waste, and reworked and reprocessed wool. The ceilings established under the regulation reflect market prices of about mid-January. The price of 64s average wool, clean basis, was fixed at $3.35 and of 64s average wool top at $4.13. The ceilings are ex-dock at port of entry, or at the seller's warehouse, regardless of country of origin, with the customary differentials for different grades.

The Defense Production Act of 1950 provides that no price ceilings shall be established or maintained for agricultural commodities at levels below the higher of parity prices or the highest prices received by producers during May 24-June 24, 1950. The Defense Production Amendments Act of 1951 adds the further provision that no price ceilings shall be established or maintained for agricultural commodities below 90 percent of prices received by producers on May 19, 1951. The price ceilings for wool established under Ceiling Price Regulation 35 are above market prices on May 19, 1951.

On May 22 OPS issued Amendment 1 to CPR-20, which fixed new ceiling prices for wool futures and wool top futures. Under this amendment, the ceiling prices at which exchange standard wool and wool tops covered by futures contracts of the Wool Associates of the New York Cotton Exchange are $3.22 per pound for wool futures and $3.895 per pound for wool top futures. The previous ceilings under CPR-20 were $3.535 and $4.265, respectively.

Revision 1 to CPR-18, issued by OPS on May 9, allows manufacturers of wool yarns and fabrics to add to their pre-Korean prices the increased cost of materials reflected in the specific ceiling prices provided in wool price regulation CPR-35 and labor cost increases up to March 1, 1951. Previously, CPR-18, issued on April 5, allowed manufacturers of wool yarn and fabric to add on dollar and cents increases in costs of labor and manufacturing material up to December 31, 1951.

CPR-45, issued June 14 established price ceilings for apparel manufacturers. The regulation permits manufacturers to add to their pre-Korean prices increases in labor and material costs up to prescribed cutoff dates.

Ceiling Price Regulation 7, issued on February 27 and subsequent amendments and revisions thereto, established ceiling prices for sales by retailers of a wide range of commodities, including apparel, blankets, drapery and upholstery fabrics, yard goods, floor coverings etc. The regulation froze percentage markups for these items as of February 24, 1951.

Table 3.- Wool, grease basis: Production in specified countries, Averages 1931-35, 1936-40 and 1941-45 annual, 1946-51

Continent and Country	Average			1946	1947	1948	1949	1950 1/	1951 1/
	1931-35	1936-40	1941-45						
	Mil.lb.	Mil.lb.	Mil.lb.	Mil.lb.	Mil.lb.	Mil.lb.	Mil.lb.	Mil.lb.	Mil.lb.
North America									
Canada	17.3	15.6	17.7	16.7	14.1	11.9	9.8	9.5	10.0
U. S.	431.1	425.3	428.5	341.8	309.4	280.5	252.5	252.5	260.0
Estimated total 2/	458.2	451.7	457.3	369.7	334.7	304.6	271.9	270.9	279.7
Europe									
United Kingdom	113.8	110.1	88.6	87.5	71.8	75.0	82.5	86.0	85.0
Eire	18.4	17.2	15.9	14.5	13.3	12.2	12.0	13.7	14.0
France	36.9	37.1	27.3	26.5	28.6	29.3	33.9	35.0	33.0
Spain	68.9	70.0	83.0	79.0	77.0	88.0	82.0	100.0	100.0
Portugal	15.8	16.3	17.2	17.6	18.0	18.0	17.0	21.2	22.0
Italy	31.0	30.4	27.5	24.7	27.1	28.9	35.3	35.0	37.0
Germany	---	31.7	35.5	25.7	25.4	26.8	23.0	27.0	27.0
Estimated total 2/ 3/	---	482.4	446.0	420.5	398.2	424.0	443.6	473.3	478.3
Soviet Union	---	310.2	279.7	287.2	285.8	304.6	314.9	325.0	335.0
Asia									
Iran	38.0	36.3	29.6	29.5	30.0	29.8	24.7	35.3	37.0
Iraq	18.5	21.6	21.1	24.2	24.2	32.7	26.7	28.7	30.0
Syria	11.1	10.7	11.0	13.3	12.7	12.1	10.0	13.0	15.0
Turkey	41.4	67.7	67.9	68.8	71.2	75.5	70.9	67.2	75.0
Afghanistan	15.0	15.0	15.0	15.0	15.0	17.0	17.2	18.0	18.0
China	90.0	88.0	81.0	75.0	75.0	75.0	75.0	75.0	75.0
India 4/	71.9	72.9	79.0	54.5	54.5	53.0	46.2	50.5	52.0
Pakistan	---	---	---	26.0	26.0	26.0	30.0	35.0	40.0
Estimated total 2/	318.1	344.2	336.7	339.6	341.8	354.7	347.2	369.5	388.9
South America									
Argentina	361.0	411.0	505.8	515.0	475.0	419.0	420.0	420.0	440.0
Brazil	35.0	35.5	37.6	44.8	43.0	45.2	48.5	47.4	49.6
Chile	33.8	32.6	38.6	38.6	41.9	41.9	46.3	44.0	46.0
Peru	18.4	19.4	17.6	17.6	15.9	17.2	18.7	19.8	20.5
Uruguay	110.6	126.2	144.0	176.0	150.3	144.0	163.3	176.4	190.0
Estimated total 2/	574.8	638.9	759.5	809.5	743.6	684.8	713.5	724.9	763.5
Africa									
Algeria	19.1	22.6	22.6	19.8	13.8	13.2	14.0	17.0	19.0
French Morocco	30.7	35.1	39.4	20.0	25.0	28.0	30.0	33.1	35.3
Tunisia	11.7	12.0	12.9	11.8	11.0	7.9	8.0	11.0	12.0
Union of South Africa	269.5	252.3	234.0	210.0	205.2	219.0	217.5	230.0	240.0
Estimated total 2/	343.1	336.8	321.9	274.4	267.8	280.0	281.4	304.5	318.4
Oceana									
Australia	1,010.5	1,051.9	1,088.0	976.8	973.0	1,031.0	1,155.0	1,177.0	1,160.0
New Zealand	281.1	313.8	350.6	367.0	362.0	367.0	390.0	372.0	380.0
Estimated total 2/	1,291.8	1,365.9	1,438.5	1,353.9	1,335.1	1,398.1	1,545.1	1,549.1	1,540.1
Estimated world total 5/	3,640.0	3,930.0	4,040.0	3,820.0	3,710.0	3,750.0	3,920.2	4,020.0	4,100.0

1/ Preliminary.
2/ Includes other countries not shown in table.
3/ Excludes U.S.S.R.
4/ Includes Pakistan prior to 1946.
5/ Rounded to tens of millions.

Compiled from reports of the Office of Foreign Agricultural Relations.

The Defense Production Amendments Act of 1951 provides that no ceiling on any material(other than an agricultural commodity) or on any service shall become effective which is below the lower of (a) the price prevailing just before the date of issuance of the regulation or order establishing such ceiling price, or (b) the price prevailing during the period January 25, 1951, to February 24, 1951, inclusive. The Act does not prohibit the establishment or maintenance of a ceiling price with respect to any material or service which (1) is based upon the highest price between January 1, 1950 and June 24, 1950, inclusive, if such ceiling price reflects adjustments for increases or decreases in costs occurring subsequent to the date on which such highest price was received and prior to July 26, 1951, or (2) is established under a regulation issued prior to the enactment of the Act.

World Wool Production
Continues to Increase

World production of apparel and carpet wool for the 1951-52 season is estimated at 4,100 million pounds, grease basis, by the Office of Foreign Agricultural Relations (table 3). This compares with the revised estimate of 4,020 million pounds for the 1950-51 season. The increase in the production of apparel wool is expected to be somewhat greater than that of carpet wool. The proportion of merino wool in the total probably will be slightly greater than during the previous season.

World wool production reached a postwar low in 1947, but has increased gradually in later years. The production estimate for the 1951 season is about 170 million pounds or about 4 percent above the 1936-40 average and only 100 million pounds below the record output of 4.2 billion pounds in 1941. The production estimate for the 1951 season, if realized, would be a new postwar high.

Production in the United States in 1950, practically all of which was apparel wool, was about 44 percent below the record of 1942. Production this year will be a little higher than last.

Production in Australia, the world's largest producer, is expected to be slightly lower, perhaps 15 to 20 million pounds or 1 to 2 percent, than the 1950-51 output. On a clean basis the percentage reduction from 1950 probably will be a little larger because of the unusually low shrinkage last season. The estimated reduction reflects a decline both in sheep numbers and the average yield per animal due to sheep drownings, pests, disease, decreased lambing, and emergency shearing. Practically the entire clip is apparel wool of which about 70 percent is merino.

Production in the Union of South Africa is expected to increase about 10 million pounds. However, production would still be only about three-fourths of the record output of 319 million pounds in 1932. Almost 90 percent of the wool produced in South Africa is apparel wool, all of which is merino.

An increase of about 8 million pounds over the 1950-51 clip of 372 million pounds is likely in New Zealand. However, even with this increase, output would still be about 10 million pounds short of the record output of 390 million pounds produced during the 1949-50 season. Practically all of the wool produced in New Zealand is apparel wool but very little of it is classified as merino or fine wool.

Production in Argentina, the largest South American producer, is estimated at 440 million pounds. This would be 20 million pounds more than last year but would be about 15 percent below the record of 515 million pounds in both 1943 and 1946. About 60 percent of the Argentine clip is classified as apparel wool, of which about 25 percent is merino.

Sheep numbers continued to increase in Uruguay last year. Wool production for the 1951-52 season is now estimated at 190 million pounds. If this estimate materializes, a new record would be established for that country. The bulk of Uruguayan production is apparel wool, about half of which is merino.

Domestic Shorn Wool
Production Increases

The quantity of wool shorn and to be shorn this year is estimated at 229 million pounds. This is 9 million pounds or 4 percent more than was shorn last year but is 41 percent less than the record of 1942.

The increase in shorn wool production this year reflects the larger number of sheep shorn and a record heavy weight per fleece. The number of sheep shorn and to be shorn is estimated at 2 percent more than the 27,150 thousand head shorn last year. The new record fleece weight of 8.23 pounds compares with the 8.11 pounds of last year.

Shorn wool production in the "native" or "fleece" wool States is estimated at 61 million pounds with an average fleece weight of 7.49 pounds. Last year 58 million pounds were shorn with an average weight per fleece of 7.36 pounds.

Production of shorn wool in the 13 Western sheep States (11 Western States, South Dakota and Texas) is estimated at 168 million pounds, about 5.5 million pounds more than in 1950. The average weight per fleece of 8.55 pounds is the second highest of record. Fleece weights in Texas averaged lower than last year, but fleece weights in the other Western States averaged the same or higher. Production declined in Texas, New Mexico, and Arizona, but increased in the other Western States.

Table 4.- Number of sheep shorn, weight per fleece and
shorn wool production, United States, 1941-51

Year	:	Number of sheep shorn 1/	: :	Weight per fleece 2/	:	Shorn wool production
	:	Thousands		Pounds		Thousand pounds
1941	.	47,722		8.12		387,520
1942	.	49,237		7.88		388,297
1943	.	47,892		7.91		378,843
1944	:	43,165		7.84		338,318
1945	.	38,763		7.94		307,949
1946	.	34,718		8.08		280,487
1947	.	31,241		8.09		252,798
1948	:	29,060		8.05		233,924
1949	:	26,975		8.04		216,873
1950	.	27,150		8.11		220,135
1951 3/	:	27,824		8.23		229,111

1/ Includes sheep shorn at commercial feeding yards.
2/ For Texas and California the weight per fleece is the amount of wool shorn
per sheep and lamb during the year.
3/ Preliminary.

Wool Stocks in United States
Continue to Decline

Stocks of apparel wool held by dealers, manufacturers, and the Commodity Credit Corporation (exclusive of wool held by CCC for the Department
of Defense) amounted to 130 million pounds, scoured basis, at the end of
the first quarter of this year (table 5). The 17 million pounds of wool
held by CCC on April 1, 1950, had been liquidated by the end of the first
quarter of this year. Private holdings showed a net increase of about 4
million; holdings of domestic wool were reduced by 20 million pounds,
while holdings of foreign wool increased 24 million pounds. Stocks in
the hands of dealers and mills on April 1 were equal to about 17.3 weeks
of consumption at the average weekly rate of the first quarter of this
year, compared with the average of 20.8 weeks for 1935-39 and about 15.2
weeks on April 1, 1950.

Stocks of carpet wool at the end of the first quarter totaled 45
million pounds, scoured basis, a reduction of 10 million pounds from a
year earlier.

Imports of Apparel Wool Increase;
Imports of Carpet Wool Decline

Imports of apparel wool have been at a substantially higher rate than
last year. During the first 5 months of 1951, imports of apparel (dutiable)
wool for consumption amounted to 143 million pounds, clean basis, or 229
million pounds, actual weight. On a clean basis, this was about 36 percent more than was imported during the same months of last year. The high
imports late last year and early this year reflected United States procure-
ment to cover military orders for wool goods.

Table 5.- Carry-over of apparel wool, scoured basis, April 1, and a
comparison of stocks with mill consumption, United States
1935-39 average and 1940-51 1/

Year	Owned by dealers and mills		Owned by United States Government		Total :reported stocks	Number of weeks mill supply represented by stocks 2/	
	Domestic wool	Foreign wool	CCC (Domestic)	DSC (Foreign)		Privately owned	Total
	1,000 pounds	1,000 pounds	1,000 pounds	1,000 pounds	1,000 pounds	Number	Number
1935-39 Average	76,588	3/ 32,587	-		3/109,175	20.8	20.8
1940	51,006	43,808			94,814	18.3	18.3
1941	44,266	70,316			114,582	12.9	12.9
1942	66,781	4/104,356		113,355	284,492	16.0	26.5
1943	59,962	86,448		168,378	314,788	12.2	26.3
1944	32,455	133,975	83,400	157,746	407,576	14.2	34.8
1945	34,378	153,946	125,600	35,553	349,477	14.7	27.2
1946	36,023	189,455	195,900		421,378	19.6	36.6
1947	51,179	159,649	193,400		404,228	18.1	34.8
1948	76,906	130,281	139,265		346,452	19.8	33.0
1949	57,705	74,872	66,744		199,321	19.9	30.0
1950	55,405	70,882	16,948		143,235	15.2	17.3
1951	35,552	94,773	5/		6/130,325	17.3	17.3

Compiled from reports of the Bureau of the Census, Commodity Credit Corporation,
and information furnished by Defense Supplies Corporation.
1/ Data are for reporting dates nearest April 1. Dates of reports range from
March 26 to April 4.
2/ Stocks compared with January-March mill consumption.
3/ Includes a small quantity of wool afloat.
4/ Excludes 36's, 40's foreign wool.
5/ Negligible.
6/ Does not include wool held by CCC for Department of Defense.

Imports of carpet wools, however, have been at a much lower rate than
last year. Imports of carpet (duty-free) wools during January-May amounted
to 61 million pounds, clean basis, or 86 million pounds, actual weight. On
a clean basis, this was about 43 percent less than the amount imported during the same months of 1950.

Apparel Wool Consumption
About Same as Last Year;
Consumption of Carpet Wool Declines

Domestic mills are consuming apparel wool at a rate only slightly lower
than last year. During January-May, woolen and worsted mills in the United
States consumed 174 million pounds of apparel wool, scoured basis. This was
at an annual rate of about 415 million pounds. Mills consumed 429 million
pounds last year. The average weekly rate for January-May was about 3 percent below that of the same period of 1950.

The rate of consumption of 60s and finer wool was about 7 percent less and of medium wools (50s up to 60s) about 2 percent less, while that of coarse wools (48s and coarser) increased 7 percent. Wools grading 60s and finer made up 56 percent of the total, 50s up to 60s made up 34 percent, and 48s and coarser wools 10 percent. Last year the percentages were 57, 33 and 10.

The rate of consumption on the woolen system increased 10 percent, while consumption on the worsted system decreased 8 percent.

Consumption of carpet wool has been at a rate substantially lower than last year. During January-May, domestic woolen and worsted mills consumed 62 million pounds, scoured basis, of carpet (duty-free imported) wool. This was at an annual rate of about 150 million pounds, compared with actual consumption of 196 million pounds during 1950. The average weekly rate during January-May was about 30 percent less than that during the same period of 1950.

Mill Output

During the first 4 months of 1951, production of yarn 1/ (other than carpet) in the United States on the woolen and worsted systems amounted to 206 million pounds. On a weekly rate basis, this represents an increase of 6 percent over last year. The rate of output of worsted yarn increased 11 percent, while the rate of spinning on the woolen system increased 3 percent. Worsted yarn production made up 42 percent of the total compared with 40 percent last year. The weekly rate of production of weaving yarn on the two systems increased 6 percent; output of knitting yarn increased 3 percent. Weaving yarn made up 84 percent of the total, the same as last year.

During the same months, domestic mills produced 67 million pounds of carpet yarn. The weekly rate during those months was about 5 percent lower than for the same period of 1950.

Production of woolen and worsted woven fabrics 2/ during the first quarter of this year totaled 96 million finished linear yards, 6 million linear yards or 6 percent less than during the first quarter of 1950. Production of woven apparel fabrics totaled 82 million finished linear yards, a decline of about 4 percent. Production of such fabrics was about equally divided between woolens and worsteds. Men's and boys' wear fabric output was down 10 percent. The quantity of fabrics produced toward Government orders was about 4 times as large as that of last year and made up 12 percent of total apparel fabric production compared with only 3 percent last year. The quantity of women's and children's wear fabric produced declined about 16 percent. Output of transportation upholstery, the major category of nonapparel fabric, declined 16 percent.

1/ Includes all yarn spun on woolen and worsted systems regardless of fiber content.
2/ Fabrics containing by weight 25 percent or more wool, reused wool, or reprocessed wool.